B WEEKEND Bear

ISBN: 978-1-998532-59-9

Published by Ahelia Publishing, LLC
PO Box 532 Augusta, MT 59410
aheliapublishing@outlook.com

Printed in United States of America
For inquiries, please contact: Ahelia Publishing @ address above.

WEEKEND
Bear

Kimm Reid, BAPsych

It was sure lonely, living on the store shelves with all the other bears. Just sitting there all day, hoping someone would take me home, was SO boring.

Every day I crossed my fingers and wished with all my wishes that somebody's mom would choose me to take home—and today—YOUR mom did!

The lady at the store put me in a bag. It was a bit dark and scary but when your mom took me to the car I peeked out because I could feel butterflies fluttering in my tummy. I bet you've had butterflies in your tummy before too.

Being outside of the store was new for me, and I had to leave all my old teddy bear friends behind. But I realized new doesn't mean bad, it just means ... different! And different is ok.

Your mom told me a secret—You have new things too. She said you sometimes live at her house, and sometimes you live at your dad's house. She said that it can be a little bit hard for you to live in two houses, so she asked me if I could go with you.

I will laugh at your jokes and soak up any sadness you might have. You can count on me, Weekend Bear, to keep your secrets and feel all your emotions with you. Emotions are ok, and sometimes you need a friend to tell your feelings to. You can tell them all to me.

So what will we do today, little Doodlebug?
We could go to the park and climb a tree.
Or maybe we should build a fort and have a
party with popcorn and lemonade!

It doesn't matter what we do,
as long as we do it together!

After my nap. we're going to your other home.
How do you feel about that?

Sometimes it's fun to have two homes.
like last week when it was your birthday.

You got two cakes and two piles of presents and two birthday parties. How fun!

You had so much fun.
didn't you. Doodlebug?

When we pack your to-go bag and get ready for change. I climb in and get comfy for the ride.

Sometimes I take a nap in the car. I'm always ready for the next adventure—you and me.

At mom's house, are some of your favorite things
that you have to leave behind sometimes.
But dad's house has some great things too,
that wait for you to come back and play with them.

But no matter which of your homes

you are at on any given day,

I am there too, little Doodlebug.

If you sometimes feel alone, you're not.
We can sing, read a story, or wish upon
stars and pretend we are lion tamers
putting on the best circus extravaganza!

At DAD's house,

we can build rocket ships from boxes,

and fly to the stars before bedtime.

At MOM's house, we can be bakers,
and make pancakes shaped like the moon!

And when you miss one house while you're at the other. I'll be right there for a squeeze and a cuddle.

You can tell me all your secrets and I'll keep them safe and sound until you feel all better.

I'll sit with you when you feel sad and you can tell me all the things that are spinning in your heart.

Good or bad, happy or mad,

Your feelings matter, every single one,

So you can trust me to hold them for you.

And no matter where we go, or what we do,
you'll always have me, Weekend Bear.

So, let's pack up our adventures, and head to the other house. Because wherever we are, it's always home, as long as we're together.

The End